MW00399528

Let's Ask Auntie Anne Series

Let's Ask Auntie Anne

How to Raise a Trusting Child

Let's Ask Auntie Anne
How to Raise a Trusting Child
Book Four

Gary and Anne Marie Ezzo
with Diane Wiggins

Let's Ask Auntie Anne
How to Raise A Trusting Child

Published by Parent-Wise Solutions, Inc. *(Parent-Wise Solutions
is a division of the Charleston Publishing Group, Inc.)*

International Standard Book Number:

1-932740-03-1

Printed in the United States of America

For information:
Parent-Wise Solutions, Inc.
2130 Cheswick Lane, Mt. Pleasant, SC 29466

04 05 06 07—7 6 5 4 3 2 1

Dedicated to…

Joey and Carla Link
There is a friend that sticks closer than a brother
(Proverbs 18:24)

Acknowledgements

Books are often a collaborative effort of many individuals whose gifts and talents help move a manuscript from scribbles to completion. This little book and the entire *Auntie Anne* series is no exception. We are indebted to a host of friends. First, we wish to thank Craig, Carly, Morgan, and Evan Wiggins for allowing wife and Mom time to work on the Auntie Anne series. Their sacrifice gave Diane the opportunity to use her creative giftedness. We also offer a hearty thank you to our wonderful editors Judith St. Pierre and Jennifer Gott. Joining them in proof reading is our dear friend Suzanne Johns and family and Michelle Warner. And last but not least, the one who inspired the completion of the series is our beloved Auntie Anne. May her Scrabble board never grow cold.

Series Prologue

Author's Notes

Meet the Real Auntie Anne

Meet the Carriage Couples

Author's Notes

In this series of books we depart from our traditional method of dialectic instruction, (premise, facts, argument and conclusion) and turn to an older and more personal style of persuasion—sharing parenting principles in story-form. Who doesn't love a good story?

Stories are entertaining and provide a unique conduit for dispensing practical wisdom and moral truth that otherwise might be lost in an academic venue. When we read or hear a story we find ourselves feeling for the characters through their speech and thoughts. We often identify and empathize with their fears, hopes, dreams and expectations. Most importantly, from their successes and failures we can learn lessons for life. Stories have the power to change us—and indeed they do!

The *Let's Ask Auntie Anne* series consist of five stories and five pertinent parenting themes. Each story is embedded with practical advice that will guide the reader to greater understanding of the complexities of childrearing and hopefully serve as a friend to motivate positive change.

Finally, the series was designed for individual or group study. The questions at the end of each book both remind and highlight the significant principles of the lessons taught. Whether you read for your own pleasure or share with a community of friends, we know you will benefit from a trip to Auntie Anne's kitchen and her treasury of parenting knowledge. Enjoy.

Gary and Anne Marie Ezzo
Mt. Pleasant, South Carolina
August 2004

Meet the Real Auntie Anne

Eleanor Roosevelt insightfully concluded that "Beautiful young people are accidents of nature, but beautiful old people are works of art." The main character in this book is, as the former First Lady described, a beautiful work of art, fashioned by the colors of life.

Auntie Anne is not a fictional character. She was born in Boston, Massachusetts, on March 24, 1914. Her life, while not as glamorous as Eleanor Roosevelt's has indeed been greatly influential. With an earthly common sense that often eludes others and a sense of humor that never fails, this amazing woman of ninety-plus years continues to endear herself to friend and stranger.

Each book in this series is as much a tribute to a beautiful life as it is a parenting resource filled with timeless wisdom and practical application. In each story (just as in real life), Auntie Anne is cheerfully spry, physically capable, neither failing in sight nor mind. A philosopher of sorts, and like those of her day, her interest extends into all areas. The mind, she believes, has no limits but those we choose to give it, and hungry minds, whether of children or the elderly, need the food of useful knowledge—*daily*.

In real life, the children who called Auntie Anne "Mom" were children of aristocrats, professors, and other notables from the fair cities up North. No, they were not her children by birth, but by design. As a Boston nanny, she loved them as a mother loves her own. She would weave buttercup crowns and sing treasured melodies. She cooked extravagantly and lusciously—spices and herbs, warm buttered bread, and crusty apple cobbler baked to a beautiful brown hue. Reading followed mealtimes routinely. Each of the children under Auntie Anne's care were taught to love books. She took them through literary adventures with Dickens, Poe, T. S. Eliot, Tolkien, Hemingway, Bunyan, and more.

The beautiful, historical City of Charleston, South Carolina, frames the backdrop for the series. Auntie Anne draws her parenting lessons from the city's rich history and the daily life of people living on or near the Carolina saltwater marshes. Charleston's glorious past from the Colonial period through the American Revolution, the Civil War, and into the present day and the beauty of its perfectly maintained historical district, cobblestone streets and waterfront parks are all woven into Auntie Anne's lessons.

From her kitchen window she overlooks the wide green marsh and the blue waters of the Wando River in the lovely neighboring town of Mt. Pleasant. The descriptions of places, scenes, and the anecdotal stories in each book are factual. Apart from Auntie Anne, the characters in our stories are fictional but their needs accurately reflect the many common concerns and challenges for today's parents. The authors speak through Auntie Anne's life story to satisfy the needs of each inquiring couple.

Come and enjoy. Put on your slippers, find a quiet nook, and benefit from a trip to RiverTowne, and Auntie Anne's kitchen. If you can picture a home by the water, a flowered paradise of sorts, with a vista of blue skies and green marshes, where birds and butterflies fill the air and the scent of ocean mingles with a Carolina morning, then you have successfully imagined Auntie Anne's home at the water's edge. Here you will find a friend, one who connects for a new generation of parents the *descriptive*—the way it was and the way it is—with the *prescriptive*—the way it should be.

Meet the Carriage Couples

I t all goes back to Missy. Of course, she could not have known the train of events to spin out of her spunky fondness for hopping in cars not her own. Nor does she own a car. This Missy, oh beg your pardon, is a dog. A fluffy white pedigree peek-a-poo with a Rottweiler complex and a James Cagney smile.

When she hopped in the car of Geoff and Ginger Portier on that Saturday night so long ago, no one could have imagined the chain of events that would eventually lead five couples on a journey of discovery about themselves and their parenting. In one of life's paradoxical moments, the beginning often becomes clearer in light of the end and so it is with our story.

It was through the strange encounter with Missy, that the Portiers first met Auntie Anne. (Narrative is found in Book Five.) It only took one delightful Sunday afternoon sipping sweet tea and playing a game of Scrabble for Geoff and Ginger to discover the treasury of Auntie Anne's knowledge.

Auntie Anne is more than a good person at heart and

a wonderful chef in the kitchen, she is also a wise sage, a woman gifted in thought with a plentiful supply of grace and charm. All of this accented by a marvelous wit. Yes, a refreshing wit that compliments her clean heart and noble mind.

In a time of desperation and perplexing challenges our dear Auntie Anne brings much needed correction and aid to Geoff and Ginger's parenting. From that experience, others would come to know of this woman's marvelous gifts.

The following Spring five couples crowded together on the padded seats of an old wooden carriage harnessed to two brown mules named Knick and Knack. Two-week-old chicks circled underfoot, pecking eagerly at feed dropped from the mules' grain bags.

A minute later, the driver shook the reins and called, "Eeyuup." Twenty-two-hundred pounds of muscle lunged forward as chicks scattered in every direction. The carriage swayed out of the big red barn to the rhythm of creaking wood and clopping hoofs. Another tour of historical Charleston, South Carolina had begun with a promise of a blessing.

Coincidence or destiny? It mattered little. It was just one of those odd occurrences in life. Five couples, strangers to each other, meet randomly on a bright and sunny Carolina morning and everything clicked. A few minutes into the carriage ride and the couples were already talking about their children left at home. School pictures traveled up and down the rows greeted by smiles and nodding heads. The tour of Charleston's historical district took just over an hour and by the time the carriage returned to the big red barn, the couples were talking like old friends. Charleston has a way of doing that, making everyone feel like family.

It was Geoff and Ginger Portier who brought up the idea of lunch. Eyes met and heads nodded and before long, five couples set out to enjoy one of the Charleston's delightful bistros. Settling in with iced chai, and a few diet cokes, the couples talked about the high points of the tour before the topic turned once again to their children, parenting and life on the home-front.

It was than that Geoff and Ginger directed the conversation by sharing what they considered to be one of Charleston's best kept secrets.

"Her name," Geoff said, "is Auntie Anne and she can change your life. Her thoughts are relevant, her searching mind insightful, and her understanding of the human heart runs deep and wide."

"She is a refreshing change from all the parenting experts I've read lately," Ginger added, "and her wise counsel is gentle and affective."

"If you need help with parenting, and find yourself frustrated with your other options, pay a little visit to Auntie Anne. There are only two things required," Geoff went on to say. "First, play a game of Scrabble with the dear woman and second, talk nice to her little dog Missy."

Geoff and Ginger continued with their celebration of Auntie Anne, sharing about that memorable Sunday afternoon months ago. The contagious energy of their enthusiasm was food for the weary soul and put hope and expectancy in the hearts of their new friends. Now peeked with curiosity and a secret longing for assistance, each couple over time would find their way to the big green house near the water's edge. The place where Auntie Anne calls home.

There are five couples and five unique parenting challenges. Listen in as Auntie Anne satisfies each inquiry with relevant and practical "rubber meets the road" advice.

In Book One, Mac and Vicki Lake can not figure out why their children act as if they are not loved. Mom and Dad are missing something so basic that even the simple phrase "I love you" falls short of its intended meaning. How well did Auntie Anne help them? You decide after reading *How to Raise a Loving Child*.

In Book Two, meet Bill and Elaine Lewis. Who doesn't know at least one family facing the frustration of irresponsible children? Messy rooms, wet towels on the floor, and unfinished homework are just the beginning. Join Bill and Elaine as they go with Auntie Anne on a journey to the heart of *How to Raise a Responsible Child*.

In Book Three, little do Rick and Lela Harvey know that a lack of security is the root of their children's behavioral problems. Nervous, irritable children acting out at school in seemingly uncontrollable ways are a dead giveaway. Auntie Anne has a plan for this home. Find out what and *who* needs to change in *How to Raise a Secure Child*.

In Book Four, Clarke and Mia Forden seek out Auntie Anne's advice on building trusting relationships. For Clarke and Mia, the pace of today's family is troubling. How will fathers capture the hearts of their children with so little time? Find out what they wished they had learned a dozen years earlier in *How to Raise a Trusting Child.*

In Book Five, Geoff and Ginger Portier tell their story of how Auntie Anne taught them how to make virtues and values real in the lives of their children. What will it take to create a love for moral beauty within the heart of their children? Auntie Anne provides solid answers in *How to Raise a Moral Child.*

Introduction

In the eyes of Clarke Forden, fatherhood has always been an impenetrable mystery. And now that he and his wife Mia, have two preteen daughters and a son about to become a teenager in a few days, his confusion over how he fits into their lives has erupted around him like gopher holes in the lawn.

Clarke is home every evening, available for talks, and involved in the kids' sports and other activities. The kids seem fine. Clarke Jr. knows when to jump and just how high to keep the folks happy. But even though they spend a lot of time doing things together, Clarke often feels as if they don't quite emotionally connect. Just a couple of years behind big brother, Wendy and Sissy usually don't come out of the woodwork until dinnertime. While they have an insider connection to Mom on girl issues, Clarke feels like a fifth wheel around them—a spare that's there but not needed until an emergency arises.

While he knows that the traditional "provide and protect" theory of fathering has gone the way of the phone booth, Clarke has never seen a satisfying picture of what a father should be. His past offers him no insights. Raised by divorced parents, he saw his dad only once a week. Who can he ask now? All the other dads he knows seem to have the same struggles.

Mia, a woman of amazing resources, had little to offer in this arena. Her dad was an overachiever and often critical of her while she was growing up. Confused and always searching for something she couldn't quite grasp, she had preferred to leave the father-daughter relationship alone. On Father's Day, she presented the requisite Old Spice After Shave, a cute card and called it a day. Now aware that her husband is searching for answers, Mia is trying hard to help. Hoping it will shed some light on this enigma, she's even taking a class on Modern Family in Society at the local community college.

Clarke feels that time is running out to cement his relationship with his kids. He has a lot of questions, as well as a mishmash of emotions he doesn't understand. Now the door of opportunity is open. Clarke and Mia are about to embark on a parenting pilgrimage to Auntie Anne's. In the inner sanctum of her kitchen, can the prophet at Mt. Pleasant reveal what's behind this mystery and illuminate the evolving role of fatherhood for this couple?

Let's see.

~ The Moment Was Here ~

Truly the moment was unnerving. Mia's insides went flippity-flop in rhythm with her familiar worn mules. Approaching the home of this stranger, she hurriedly prayed that Auntie Anne was not one of those shoes-off-at-the-front-door kind of people. "I don't have socks," she mumbled to no one in particular.

Her tall, broad-shouldered husband responded only with a glance. Clarke mentally reviewed the events leading up to this strange encounter. Laughing quietly to himself, he imagined going home and telling the guys at the office how a group of strangers bonded on a carriage tour of Old Towne Charleston and one by one, they all paid homage to a ninety-year-old sage. Maybe some stories are better left unsaid.

Clarke looked at the decorative green and white porcelain house number and then back to his scribbled directions. "This is it Mia," he confirmed as his eyes took in the freshly painted soft green home with black hurricane shutters open to the late afternoon breeze.

The two followed the walkway to the front steps. Mia paused a moment to survey the landscaped garden. From behind a large spray of Lady Bank roses, a truffle-colored bird warbled a magical tune catching Mia's attention. The music was comforting, like a prelude of a blessing to come. Glancing up, Mia's eyes focused on four white wooden rockers that seemed inviting and friendly.

Climbing the ten triple-wide steps, Clarke felt the strong, sturdy wooden planks beneath his feet and paused to examine the construction. Not yet able to move, Mia stared at the huge, shiny black door in front of her. A heart-shaped wreath erupted with a burst of color, complementing the azalea blooms on either side of the steps. Mounted on the left side of the doorframe was a small brass figure of a twelfth-century monk grasping a thick, black chain attached to a small bell.

Lela, one of the engaging wives Mia met on the carriage tour, had told her about the monk and said that it had some kind of symbolic importance for her. Mia almost felt that she was standing at the entrance to a church. Inspired by the thought, she climbed the steps, paused at the top, and then pulled the chain.

From behind the door came the sounds of a small dog announcing their presence.

"Hush Missy," a voice said. The tone was firm, but not sharp. With the sound of steel against steel, the front bolt slid back, the door swung wide. There, standing before them was Auntie Anne. She was wearing a short-sleeved blue smock the color of a perfect summer sky.

"Hello, Auntie Anne. We're Clarke and Mia Forden, friends of Geoff and Ginger."

"Yes, yes, come in. I've been expecting you. Geoff rang last night and said you'd be coming by this after-noon. Did you have any problem finding the place?" Auntie Anne asked directing her questions to Clarke.

"Oh, no problems at all," Clarke said. "The directions were very clear."

"By the way," Mia interjected, "Elaine Lewis sends her greetings to you. I spoke with her earlier this week. She is so excited that we are finally going to meet."

"Bill and Elaine. What a sweet couple. I so enjoyed getting to know them. Well, please come in," Auntie Anne beckoned with her hand.

Clarke and Mia stepped inside to a comfortable entry hall. Auntie Anne's eyes lingered momentarily at the deep yellow Confederate Jasmine winding its way through the porch spindles. Across the way, Miss Nancy gave a wave catching her attention. Auntie Anne waved back, making a mental note to call later and ask her husband Harold to bring home a doorstop from the hardware store he managed in town.

She turned her attention back to her guests. Clarke was a handsome young man, a tad thin but possessing a kind face. Mia appeared to be several years younger, possibly in her mid-thirties. Auntie Anne noticed how she glanced around nervously, intermittently biting her lower lip. Her shoulder-length brown hair sported the trendy layering like Auntie Anne had seen around town.

Over all, the couple was an engaging pair, with a vulnerable openness in their eyes that left Auntie Anne glad they had come. If nothing else, she would fill their tummies with good food, and comfort their souls with tales of survival.

"Auntie Anne, it's so nice to meet you." Clarke said, extending his hand.

Auntie Anne reached out to take Clarke's hand. Then standing on her tiptoes she offered him a warm hug. "Well, I was hoping it would be," she said with a bright smile. She then turned and extended both arms to embrace Mia.

"Mia… such a fine name, It's Hebrew, I think. Yes. I believe it means 'Who can compare with God?' A beautiful meaning for a name."

"Yes, that is what it means, Auntie Anne," Mia said, "How did you know?" A whiff of gardenia wafted past Mia like incense as Auntie Anne stepped back. Her eyes were a deep blue, and now they churned like the water off the South Carolina coast. She seemed to see everything.

"Oh, I like to learn about names," she said. "They're kind of like pets. They tell you something about their owners."

Clarke looked down. Missy was dancing in circles on her hind feet, demanding to be introduced. In a surprising display of agility for someone approaching the century mark, Auntie Anne bent down and swooped up the little dog in her arms. "You need to see them up close and personal, don't you?" she said. Missy began sniffing the guests.

It was then that Mia noticed the loosely woven slippers on Auntie Anne's feet. They looked so cool and comfortable. Auntie Anne picking up on Mia's glance motioned toward a small deacon's bench. Sitting on top, a round basket made from sweetgrass native to the Carolina coast held knitted slippers in a variety of colors. "I knit them for the comfort of our visitors," she said. "Please Mia, help yourself to a pair." She made it sound like a prerequisite for the visit, so right then and there Mia slipped off her brown leather mules and donned the colorful footwear.

Clarke took notice of the basket for the first time. "Is that a sweetgrass basket, like the ones the locals make?"

"Yes, it is Clarke. Isn't it beautiful?" Auntie Anne said as she held the basket out and turned it in her hand. "You know, sweet grass basket making has been around Mt. Pleasant for more than three hundred and thirty years. The baskets were such a vital part of plantation life. The art came with the slave trade from West Africa, and the descendants have been making baskets like this ever since. I have another one in the kitchen."

Just then three loud beeps sounded. "Coffee's brewed!" Auntie Anne said. She bent over, set Missy back on the floor, and headed in the direction of the kitchen. "Join me please in the kitchen."

They entered the kitchen to the gurgling sound of the coffee pot as the last drops of water pushed through the filter. Clarke and Mia were invited to sit at a cozy table decorated with a lace tablecloth. With the back drop-leaf down, the table sat flush against three windows overlooking a panoramic view of the marsh and the sparkling blue water beyond.

Auntie Anne set three plain white coffee cups on the table and then paused. "I'm sorry, I should know this but, where do you kids call home?"

"Ohio," Clarke replied.

"Oh, yes. Ginger mentioned that."

"We live just outside of Cincinnati in a little town called Merrimont," Mia added.

"Merrimont." Auntie Anne rolled the name around in her mind. "It means 'a merry mountain.' With a name like that, it must be a great place to raise children." She walked to the coffee pot and returned to the table with the carafe. "Have some?" she asked Clarke.

"Which?" Clarke said. "Some coffee or some kids?"

"Why, children of course." Auntie Anne laughed. "You didn't come all this way just for coffee, did you?"

Clarke and Mia smiled, comforted by Auntie Anne's wit.

"Auntie Anne, to answer your question, we *do* have children," Clarke said. "Three of them. Clarke Jr. is twelve; well, he will be thirteen in a few weeks. Wendy is ten and Sissy is eight-and-a-half."

Mia glanced at Clarke and back to Auntie Anne.

"They're one reason we're here today," she said. "The other is to meet you. We have heard so much about you from the carriage couples. Elaine Lewis says she's moving in with you, and Ginger is trying to get Geoff transferred back to Charleston."

"Oh, what sweet people they are. I miss Geoff and Ginger not living close by."

"They miss you, too, Auntie Anne," Clarke said. "They talk about you all the time."

"Ginger mentioned that you used to be a governess up North," Mia said. "That must have been very rewarding."

"Yes it was. Those are some of my fondest memories. I loved all those children as my very own, and many of them still come by to see me. They tell me that even though Charleston is a long way from Boston, it's like coming home."

Auntie Anne rose from the table and walked over to the kitchen island. She stopped and picked up a bunch of overripe bananas out of a large basket and held them up "Just look at what the heat has done to these things. I was going to bake some of my special banana-nut muffins today. There are enough here for a double batch. But, the oven is no friend on a hot day."

Mia offered an understanding nod, from one chief

to another.

Clarke took notice of the empty basket. "Is that another one of those sweet grass baskets, Auntie Anne?"

"Yes it is. This is a great one for holding fruit with its flared edges. It's beautifully fitted together. Attractive isn't it?" Clarke nodded affirmingly." "May I look at it?"

Auntie Anne handed the basket to Clarke. His fingers roamed the smooth, firm weave, a mixture of sweet grass for the light weave, bull rushes for the dark weave, and palmetto strips holding it all together. Touching it made him appreciate the mind that had envisioned it. Every weave was purposeful.

Auntie Anne walked over and opened the refrigerator. She turned back to her guests, "As hot as it is, I decided to save my baking for later. So, I thought you might enjoy this instead." She returned to the table with a pie tin filled with something chocolaty. "Will you try a piece of this?"

"Oohhh," Mia said. "Is that a chocolate mousse pie? That would be my all-time favorite. But, oh my, the calories! I guess I'd better have just a smidgen." Mia placed her thumb close to her forefinger to indicate how much.

Auntie Anne set the pie on the table and cut a small piece.

"Ah, Auntie Anne. Calories don't bother me," Clarke said eyeing the sweet temptation. "You can put the rest of Mia's share on my plate. With all the time I spend running back and forth between the kids' games, I'll burn up those calories before they even get near the fat cells."

Auntie Anne smiled and moved her pie knife over to make a wide slice. "Will this do Clark?"

Clark's head nodded as his eyes grew wide. "That will do just fine Auntie Anne." His gaze meanwhile, returned to the basket. Intrigued by its design, he began to study it. "There is such perfection in this weave; it's hard to imagine each basket is hand-made."

"Every one of them," Auntie Anne replied, "and for

the last three hundred years, most have been fashioned by women."

Mia gave Auntie Anne a questioning look. "I thought it was always that way, you know, a craft passed from mother to daughter to granddaughter."

"Well, actually that was not the way it started. Way back in Africa, this was a fatherly art. Fathers passed on their skills to their sons and daughters. Today, a few men are involved, but it's no longer the fatherly directed craft it once was."

"When did it change Auntie Anne?" Clarke asked as he set the basket down.

"It happened as the plantations were drawn into the growing market economy. The plantation owners would outsource the men to other jobs, working the rice fields, planting and harvesting, things like that. Competition for the father's time and energy did not leave room for much else, especially the intricacy of this art. In time the knowledge of basket weaving fell entirely to the women. Now every sweetgrass basket is fashioned by a mother's caring hand.

Auntie Anne paused to emphasis her conclusion. Clarke and Mia were attentive. "Missing unfortunately," she continued, "is a father's special touch. Much like today's family. There are too many things competing for dear ol' dad's attention."

Clarke thought about this for an instant. "That's an interesting analogy Auntie Anne. Too many things competing. It sounds like you're onto something. What do you think Mia?"

Mia mused a moment over Auntie Anne's words. Turning to Clarke she slowly shared her thoughts. "Well, fathers do seem overly wrapped up in getting to T-ball one night and soccer practice three nights a week and gymnastics on Saturday morning. Something seems out of balance. There are a lot of things competing for time and our children's attention. Even I notice it."

"Maybe that's why so many fathers are training their children from the sidelines of soccer fields, basketball courts, and baseball diamonds," Clarke thought out loud. "Actually, now that I think about it, they're not training at all. Are they? They're just spectators in their children's world."

The conversation temporarily went on hold as Auntie Anne removed the basket and placed it back on the counter. She handed Clark his piece of pie and then served herself. Everyone took a few bites. Missy immediately came alive. She knew that food on the table translated to crumbs on the floor.

"Auntie Anne, is there any hope for a burdensome

father? I know with three kids I'm pulled in so many directions between school, sports and church activities. What should stay and what should go?"

Auntie Anne put her fork across her plate. She lifted her cup and cradled it with two hands. "The tension you face Clarke is brought on by too much competition in your children's world."

"Oh, I couldn't agree with you more, Auntie Anne." The words burst from Mia's lips. "I've never thought it was a good idea to rush young children into competitive sports. Their emotions are much too immature to handle the intensity of competition. Don't you agree?"

"I do agree Mia, but the kind of competition I was referring to creates a more subtle danger."

Not quite sure what to expect or where this conversation was headed, Clarke and Mia gave Auntie Anne their full attention. It was apparent that, unlike many elderly people, she wasn't buried in the past or bamboozled by the present. She paid attention to what was going on and had clear insights into the changing world. Clarke and Mia were about to discover just how much of a grasp Auntie Anne had on reality.

"We would love to hear your thoughts on this Auntie Anne," Clarke asked nearly pleading.

"I have a few thoughts I can share, but right now,

how about a calming game of Scrabble?"

"Calming game said the spider to the fly? We heard from Mac and Vicki and Bill and Elaine all about your scrabble victories Auntie Anne. I don't know if 'calming' is the best word to describe what you do to your opponents," Clarke said as he turned his smile toward Mia.

"Well, I'm up for a game Mia said enthusiastically. But promise Auntie Anne that we can finish our discussion about competition."

"Oh, we will do that Mia. I promise." Auntie Anne walked over to the old kitchen Hoosier and removed a long flat red box, with faded gold lettering. She brought the box to the table and set it on the Lazy Susan. The board was set up and tiles retrieved from the blue velvet bag.

"Who's first?" Clarke asked.

"Easy big guy." Mia patted Clarke's arm. "You haven't even looked at your letters. Auntie Anne, why don't you start the game for us?"

"I will, but please, do not let my nephew know we started this way. He insists that we play by the rules. I can't get away with anything when he's around." At this, Auntie Anne broke out in a smile and then laughed at her own statement. Mia joined in her light heartedness.

Auntie Anne began to shuffle a few letters here and

there and then placed the simple word *barn* on the board. "Not many points, but it's enough to get the game started."

Mia placed *limp* down the board underneath the *b*, catching Clarke unprepared. The ladies fussed with the new tiles on their trays, trying to look busy while he came up with a word.

"Okay, you caught me," Clarke mumbled.

Missy ceased her crumb patrol, jumped onto the seat next to Auntie Anne, and curled up.

"Ah ha! Here we go. How about some *money*?" Clarke placed *oney* next to Mia's *m*."

When her turn came around again, Auntie Anne added *acles* to the end of *barn* to make the word *barnacles*.

"Wow, that's pretty clever, Auntie Anne. A double word score too," Clarke said with a tinge of envy.

"What are barnacles anyway?" Mia asked. "Everyone down here is so concerned about getting them in their boats."

"Not *in* their boats Mia, *on* their boats," Clarke corrected. Barnacles attach themselves to the bottom of boats that are left in the salt water. That's why boats down here are on lifts. If they are moored in the water, barnacles build up on the hull. I guess barnacles really don't serve any useful purpose in nature.

"Actually Clarke" Auntie Anne began to speak while wiping a drop from the side of her cup. "Barnacles are tiny living creatures that serve an important purpose in the cycle of marine life. They are a plentiful food source for fish and other crustaceans, and they provide structure for fish habitats. But like so many other things, their natural capacity for good can also destroy."

"I always struggle with that type of paradox," Clarke said. "How can something good become bad, or destructive?"

"Well, in the case of a boat, it is the subtle, accumulative weight of barnacles on the hull that interferes with the boat's ability to navigate. The boat cannot cut through the water the way it was designed to do so. Barnacles make navigating difficult and dangerous. If they aren't removed, their cumulative weight can swamp a boat or even sink it. Every once in a while people come across a beached boat with its hull damaged because of these little creatures."

"It's hard to imagine that tiny little crustaceans weighing a fraction of an ounce can accumulate to the point of sinking a boat," Clarke said. "Talk about a subtle danger."

"Subtle danger is right," Auntie Anne said. "Just like competition and fathering in a new millennium.

"I'm sorry," Mia said truly apologetic. I'm finding this conversation very interesting, but I'm confused. The subtle danger of good becomes bad and barnacles swamping a boat. How does this relate to competition and fathering?"

"Well Mia, like the subtle effects of barnacles, our society has accumulated some social barnacles that makes it very difficult for parents to navigate a proper course for nurturing children."

"Would one of those barnacles happen to be competition, Auntie Anne?" Mia asked, hoping her understanding was catching up to Clarke's.

"Yes it is. Auntie Anne said with a firm nod. "Our society has formed a confusing web of competing values that clandestinely war against the family and in particular, fathering. You see, when good wars with evil you at least know who your enemy is. You're able to draw your battle lines, assess your strengths and weaknesses. You can reinforce your defenses and develop a strategy for victory. The lines between the two are clear cut. But when good competes against good all sense of caution is lost."

Auntie Anne paused to sip her coffee and allow her words to sink in.

"As a society, we have a few blind spots born out of our noble way of thinking. One is the belief that nothing bad can come out of something good. It's very easy for today's parents to get lost in pursuit of many opportunities offered by 'good things'. Many good values compete against other good values for supremacy in our families. So it's easy for parents to wander off course, even as they are pursing good things for their children."

Pausing for a moment, Auntie Anne looked over to Clarke and Mia. "Did I lose you kids?"

Clarke and Mia smiled, more intrigued than confused. Already it was clear what the other carriage couples were talking about. Auntie Anne saw more than other people did and she was more than capable of reading the tea leaves of the day.

~ To know more, do more, have more ~

"I follow your premise up to a point," Clarke said. "But…" he paused wanting to present his question respectfully. He had no desire to challenge or dismiss her words, but only hoped to better understand them. "How can something that is intrinsically or naturally good, become bad?"

"It happens when good values compete for supremacy over other good values denying the best values opportunity to serve."

Auntie Anne paused, fearful that she had not sufficiently prepared the ground to receive the seeds of new thought. "Let me say it this way. Our wonderful society is driven by three marketplace forces: science, technology and economics. Science leads us to technology and technology drives our economy."

Mia looked puzzled. "I don't understand what your saying Auntie Anne. Science, technology, and economics, aren't they the bedrock of our society? How can they be bad? And how do they impact fathering?"

"Oh, the impact is there, subtle though it may be," she said. "Independently, science, technology and marketplace economics are not bad, but when they are linked together, the three begin to push out other good values. Science presses us to know more, technology makes the way for us to do more, and together, economics creates the right conditions for us to have more."*

Clarke and Mia smiled, slightly overwhelmed by what they were hearing. The other carriage couples said Auntie Anne possessed an acute awareness of contemporary social issues, but this discussion went way beyond their expectation. Actually it went way beyond their own awareness of the times.

"For example," Auntie Anne continued. "If you kids will allow me to probe a little into your family and past as children. . ."

Clarke and Mia looked at each other and then back to Auntie Anne."Please go ahead," Clarke said.

*Auntie Anne's commentary on the three dominant social forces adapted from the work of Jim Petersen & Mike Shamy. Their thesis is further developed in *The Insider*, Nav Press, Colorado Springs, CO 2003.

"Thank you," she said with a slow nod. "How would you compare your children's toy box with the one you had as kids?"

"That's easy," Clarke said. "I didn't have a toy box."

"Why not?" Auntie Anne asked.

" Well… ahh… because… because I didn't have all the toys my kids have. As kids we spent more time letting our imaginations direct our fun. I remember once my dad helped me carve a wooden rifle from a dead branch. And we used to make kites out of newspaper and the neatest boats from discarded blocks of wood."

"What about you, Mia?" Auntie Anne asked.

"Hmmm…. Now that you mention it, most of the things we called toys were of the makeshift type. We had as much fun learning to make doll dresses as we did playing with our dolls. I remember that when I was six, our favorite plaything was a big refrigerator box in our basement. Oh, the adventures we had in that thing!" A bright smile warmed Mia's face. "Mom and Dad played a lot of board games with us, too, and we went on more picnics than families do today."

"Do you see what has happened, Mia?" Auntie Anne asked."Science, technology, and economics have combined to make it possible for your children to have lots of sophisticated toys and activities. But in the process many values once deemed important—like playing board games, going on picnics together, or making a toy rifle from a tree branch with dad—have been left behind. The values of knowing more, doing more, and having more begin to compete with the value of being more, and to achieve the first three, we start outsourcing our relationship with our kids and replacing them with activities."

Mia turned to look at Clarke. "Could we be out-sourcing our kids' relationship?" she said, no longer smiling. "What, with school, all the sports activities and your job, we seem scattered, going in every direction." Mia's speech slowed as she realized she was describing the very point Auntie Anne was making. "Oh, my!" Mia said, almost startling herself. "To know more, to do more; to have more—all good values, but all compet-ing with being more. Activities have become a substi-tute for us."

"I think you're getting my point, dear," Auntie Anne said softly. Good activities become a substitute for a trusting relationship. And that is where father's today are failing. If they can get the trust thing right, then activities will find their proper resting place.

"Huh. It's almost like we reversed that Clarke," Mia said looking over to her bewildered husband.

Clarke looked up from his tray. "I'm not sure Mia, where to begin to turn this around. Auntie Anne, is there any hope?"

"Oh there is Clarke. Start with the fundamentals. The good Lord has let my eyes observe the coming and going of five generations of family," she said. "While many things have changed since I was young, the basic needs of children have not. All children need to know that they belong and feel loved. Trust is the bridge that links this need with its fulfillment. Trust is the bridge of all human relationships. So building a bridge of trust with your children Clarke, should be your first value, with time and outside activities playing a supportive role. The fact is that the quality and quantity of trust your children have in you is ultimately the only true bench-mark measuring your relationship with them."

Missy was perched on the edge of the chair, look-ing for a bridge to her best friend's lap. Reaching out, Auntie Anne made the transfer. Then she plunged her thick fingers into Missy's long white hair and began to slowly stroke her up and down and back up again.

"This is making sense to me," Mia said. "As parents we get so busy learning more, doing more, and having more that we begin to... what?... fill blocks of time with activities instead of building a trusting relationship with them? Would that be a fair way to summarize it, Auntie Anne?"

Auntie Anne slowly nodded her agreement. That is exactly what happens Mia."

"I see this happening in our family," Clarke added. "Our lives are filled with time-absorbing activities. They're not bad activities. In fact, most are good. But when you think about it, they don't seem to be building up our relationship with the kids. When they're over, they're over, and our relationships aren't any better off for all the time invested."

Clarke paused, momentarily contemplating his own conclusion. He turned his gaze toward Auntie Anne. "How can we tell the difference Auntie Anne? How does a father know if he is building a trusting relationship with his children or just filling time with activities? Where does he begin to build that bridge of trust?"

"Those are all good questions Clarke, but I would like to put them on hold for just a moment to ask another important question for where we are at right now."

Clarke senses went on alert. "Go ahead Auntie Anne, I'm ready. Fire away."

"Do you have a word that you can play on the board, because Mia and I are waiting for you?"

"Oh, sorry about that," Clarke said as he began to

fumble with his letters, shifting them back and forth. Mia, held back a chuckle. It felt good to smile.

Clarke paused for a second and then picked three tiles off the tray, "It's not much but I'll go with *sow*." He played his letters and watched as Auntie Anne added up his score. So far, Auntie Anne had provided him with a unique perspective on competing values, and he had asked a lot of questions. But he still didn't have concrete answers as to how he should go about building a bridge of trust to his children. Even so, he felt it would only be a matter of time before he found out.

Auntie Anne had no sooner put the word *trait* on the board and penciled her score, when she stood up. "Let's put the game on hold for a moment. I want to show you kids something out back. It will only take a minute."

Auntie Anne was off across the kitchen and halfway to the back door before Clarke was out of his chair. Hurrying to keep up, Mia almost tripped over Missy, who rolled onto her back thinking she would get her tummy scratched. Mia stopped, bent over and rubbed Missy a few times, and then chased after Clarke and Auntie Anne. Missy followed Mia hoping for more.

Four white pillars framed the back piazza. Through each space, Auntie Anne overlooked a stunning view of a meticulously landscaped common, bursting with design, color and freshly mowed lawn that gave a golf-course feel to the place. Beyond the common came the deep green marsh and sparkling blue water. "Look around for a moment," Auntie Anne pointed with the sweep of her hand, "and tell me what you see."

Punctuated by park benches under willow trees, the lush green common was surrounded by a cinder foot-path that itself was outlined by a double row of red bricks. A delightful profusion of flowers added depth and height to the walkway. Beds of purple and blue pansies, pink petunias, and orange and white lantana ran along the sides. Here and there where magnolia trees, perfectly positioned, with their white silky blossoms in full bloom. Deep indigo blue violas and vivid orange marigold accented their base.

"It looks like a snapshot of the Promised Land." Clarke said. "Someone certainly gave some thought to the design of this place. It's peaceful, soothing to the eye, even refreshing to the soul."

Auntie Anne continued gazing out at the common. "It's amazing what you can do with a field."

"Well, this is far from being a field," Mia said with

a curious look at Auntie Anne. "It's more like a botanical garden walk."

"So it is Mia," Auntie Anne said. "But only because the parts were fitted together just right to make the whole. If the grass wasn't mowed, it would just be a field. If it didn't have a footpath, it would only be a lawn. And if the pathway didn't have flowers, it would only be a trail. The beauty is in the details, the little things. You see, the broad sweep of the landscaped lawn is lovely, but it's the pansies poking through a sidewalk that packs the punch. And that's what every father must stay mindful of."

Auntie Anne turned her gaze to Clarke. "It's the little things fathers do that count the most in their relationship with their children. The little details are what make common things beautiful."

Clarke and Mia just stared at Auntie Anne, soaking in the wisdom of her insights. They looked again at the small details that gave the common its beauty. They missed these details at first, but now they could see the relevancy of their influence. Her point made, Auntie Anne turned to the back door, beckoning her visitors to follow.

~ The Importance of Belonging ~

The trio returned to the game. Missy began wandering around the kitchen like a bored toddler needing direction.

Mia placed *think* on the board, and then Clarke added *ed* to *sow*. Auntie Anne packed seven letters together. A shuffle here and a slide there, and then intersecting with the *d* in *sowed*, she placed *identity* on the board.

Clarke looked at the board in amazement. "Auntie Anne you used all your letters! That's a fifty-point bonus. I'll never catch you now."

"Sure you can. Just clear your tray once," she quickly offered hope as if it was an easy task. "I'll add up my points but I want you kids to think about what it is about Charleston that captivates you."

Clarke looked at Mia, studying her face and then turned back to Auntie Anne working her pencil and score furiously. "History, I think. It's all about the past: the architecture, the forts, plantations, the customs, gardens and Southern gentility."

"Oh, Clarke, it's so much more than that" Mia said with a bit of frustration in her voice. "History is definitely a strong facet, but what about the shear character and personality of Charleston? Walk down any street in the historic district and you fall in love with the place. The beauty of the flowers, wrought-iron gates, and fences draped with vines of every color and variety, the secret gardens, classic details of the single houses snuggled next to each other with their grand white piazzas, and the cobblestone streets, all those little details have a way of mesmerizing you.

"I guess it represents something established, tested by time," Clarke added. "It instills a sense of belonging. Do you know what I mean Auntie Anne?"

"Yes I do Clarke. It is a city that makes you want to belong because it's been through so much and a person can find comfort and security in its strengths. We who live here belong to Charleston as much as Charleston belongs to us."

"Belonging, Auntie Anne. I guess that was your point in the first place, wasn't it," Mia asked with a newly discovered conviction. "No amount of activities can make a child feel as if he belongs to a family. Something more is required. Busyness is no substitute for belonging."

"You are very perceptive Mia. Part of the great enjoyment of belonging is the *esprit de corp* that makes up the city and the same is true with your family. Your kids need to hear from you how excited you are about the family. I promise you, whenever a dad is excited about the family, then the children get excited about the family. This is what helps build a healthy family identity and deepens their level of trust in their father."

Clarke fussed over his letters while he tried to recall if he had ever told his own children how he felt about their family. It was there, in his heart, but had he ever communicated it to the kids? Had he ever said something as simple as 'This is a great family' or 'I'm so excited to be part of this family' or 'You kids are so lucky to have such a great mom.' Using simple phrases to create a climate of identity and belonging, how hard could that be?

~ The Importance of Words ~

For a while the only sound was an occasional snort or dreamy bark from Missy. As each player scrutinized the field for easy points, words continued to fill the board. A prefix here, a plural there. Auntie Anne placed the word *venue* on the board, with the *v* on a triple letter score.

"Auntie Anne, that one little letter is worth a bunch

of points."

Auntie Anne glanced at the board and then at Clarke. "Sometimes it's the little things that have the greatest value."

"Like pansies popping up along the walkway?" Mia said reciting the earlier lesson.

"Yes Mia, Auntie Anne said to her star student. "But also like little letters." She pointed to the board. "Letters make words, and words make memories."

Clarke pondered Auntie Anne's words and was lost in thought. Throughout history the written word has recorded emotions that otherwise would be lost forever. How many times had he missed little opportunities to capture with words the history of his own family? Glancing over at Missy's little portable kennel, Clarke noticed the words "Missy's Retreat" etched over the small opening. "Words," he said, "meet our deep need to belong."

"Indeed," said Auntie Anne "Words are keys to building trust with children. Not just hearing them, but seeing them in writing. That's one way you inscribe them on your children's hearts. Words are important because they can go where Dad can't always be."

"I like that Auntie Anne," Mia said. "Words go where Dad can't always be."

"Yes, for example in a school lunchbox."

"Lunchbox, Auntie Anne?" Her statement took Clarke and Mia by surprise. "I thought we were talking about using words to preserve history, pass on memories, and promote family identity."

"Words will do that Clarke," Auntie Anne said lifting her eyes from her tray. "But parents underestimate the influencing power of their own words. Words can build a sense of belonging and identity—or they can tear down. Words of a Mom or Dad can fashion the destiny of a child as much as anything.

Clarke now fully attentive to Auntie Anne, mentally left the Scrabble game behind.

"One of the surest ways of letting children know they belong in your world" Auntie Anne continued "is to routinely write them a note. Not an e-mail Clarke, but a handwritten note from you. Place it in their lunchbox so they'll read it at school. Just say you're thinking about them or tell them what a fun time you had with them recently and that you can't wait to see them when you get home. I guarantee, while your children may discard and lose interest in other letters, they'll keep a love note from their father."

"So Auntie Anne, if my words can go with my children when I can't, putting notes in their lunchboxes is one way I can multiply my influence as a dad. Right?"

"It is indeed, Clarke. It is indeed!" Think of how many children wish they had just one hand written love note from their fathers? What I'm suggesting is note and letter writing become a way of life for you. Give your children a memory of dad. Your words can go where often you cannot."

~ The Importance of Touch ~

"Auntie Anne, all this thinking is burning up so many calories, may I please have another piece of pie?" Mia asked with a smile. "A sliver of course."

"Oh, I'm feeling so weak Auntie Anne," Clarke said with his little boy grin. "Is there a small piece for me?"

Auntie Anne laughed at both of them. "I would be delighted." Serving her guests she asked with a reassuring smile, "have you ever considered the physical side of trust?"

"Trust has a physical side to it?" Clarke asked pausing with a piece of pie half-way to his mouth. "I've never really thought about trust like that. I mean, Mia is the hugger in our family and she does a good job at it. She's always hugging those kids. I do a lot with my kids to show them I love them, but I admit, I probably fall short in the hugging department."

"You know Clarke, your father wasn't a big hugger either," Mia said. "Maybe his father didn't hug him. It's kind of like those sweetgrass baskets—somewhere in the Forden family past, the male hugging thing stopped."

Clarke listened attentively, as much with his heart as his ears. "You see Clarke," Auntie Anne continued, "within the family, a gentle hand, a tender hug, a pat on the back, and a goodnight kiss all communicate intimacy in a relationship." Her blue eyes spoke as clearly as her voice. "To hold Wendy, Sissy and Clarke Jr. and be held by them, communicates vulnerability and closeness that no one else can offer like a caring dad. There is no substitute for a father's arms."

"Not even Mia's?"

"Not even Mia's Clarke! A mother's touch provides comfort. A father's touch provides security. That is the difference, and it is a big difference!" Auntie Anne's voice was strong, yet gentle, accompanied by a sense of urgency for her guests. Clarke sat back contemplating the message.

"Most children know their father by his voice and his actions, but how many children know him by his loving touch? It's another one of the little details Clarke that makes what is common, beautiful." Looking over at Mia, Auntie Anne added, "This is part of the bridge building process that fathers can't afford to pass off to moms." Mia nodded her full agreement.

Suddenly, Clarke wanted to be held by his own father, deceased now ten years. How much could he remember? He strained to recapture the memory of even one embrace. Surely his father had held him. But had he done it enough? Can a father ever hold his children too much or too long?

~ The Importance of Guarding Your Tongue and Tone ~

As the sun moved toward the western horizon, monster cotton ball clouds were threatened by a darkening sky. Soon thunder rumbled in the distance and a summer thundershower passed through Mt. Pleasant on its way out to sea. The storm was over as quickly as it began.

Missy, who had taken refuge under the table at the first sound of thunder, now sat at Auntie Anne's feet making soft pleading puppy sounds.

"Oh, so now that its cooler, you want to go out, do you? Okay, Missy. I'll let you out," Auntie Anne crossed the room to the back door. "There you go."

She returned to her chair and the three sat watching as Missy darted down the back stairs, in a big hurry to go nowhere. She crisscrossed the yard, sniffing, and tilting her furry little head in response to every sound.

"Well then, I guess we'd better finish this game," Auntie Anne said directing her guest's attention back to the board.

It seemed to Clarke that the teaching was over. He was resolved to build a bridge of trust to his children, and he knew what needed to be done. What more could there be? Content with all he had learned and eager to put it in practice, he threw himself back into the game. He knew he couldn't pull out a win at this point, but he might still beat Mia.

At that moment, Missy appeared outside the door, dancing around and making small sounds, seeking entrance. Mia rose and let her in. Once inside, Missy ran to the middle of the room, stamped her muddy paws, and gave her wet coat a shake. In her mouth she clenched a green, half-open bud from a magnolia tree.

"Now, what did you bring to show me?" Auntie Anne asked, leaning forward in her chair. Missy danced at her feet, still grasping the bud in her teeth. Entering into the joy of Missy's moment, Auntie Anne clapped her hands. "What a beautiful find, Missy!" she said. Reveling in the praise, Missy moved her tail into high gear.

Mia's eyes moved from Auntie Anne to the bundle of damp brownish white puppy, to the devastation Hurricane Missy had wrought on Auntie Anne's spotless kitchen. "So," she said," you just overlook the mud and the water and the little paw prints?"

"I don't overlook them," Auntie Anne said." I just don't draw attention to them."

"Until when?"

"Until the moment is past and all the joy has been absorbed. Until I don't want to scream any more." Auntie Anne laughed and grabbed a handful of her hair as if she were about to yank it out. "A little mud isn't worth squashing the joy."

Missy lay down in her small round basket with the prized magnolia bud safe within paw's reach. Lifting her head and tilting it slightly, she looked at her beloved friend. "You accept me and my gifts," she seemed to say.

Clarke couldn't help but think that Auntie Anne treated her dog with more patience and understanding than he sometimes treated his own kids. He slumped a little in his chair. "I'm afraid I've missed many a magnolia bud in my time. Just the other day Sissy came running in the house with a couple of crayfish she caught and put them on the table. She was dancing around in excitement, but the crayfish had sand and pond mud on them, and I just yelled at her to get them off the table. She was sharing the joy of her discovery with me and I rejected it all because of a little dirt. I still remember the look on her face. Even now my heart aches at the thought."

Looking over with eyes of understanding, Auntie Anne began to share. "Our children are just like little puppies sometimes. Figuratively speaking of course," she added with a smile for clarity. "They have so much confidence in our acceptance of who they are, that when they find a treasure they want to run and share their moment of discovery with us, even if it's just an oversized pine cone, a special colored rock, or the first Autumn leaf."

"Or a new hairdo, Clarke," Mia's eyes met his. Clarke looked like a reprimanded puppy.

"Mia means that when Wendy came home with her hair newly permed, I wasn't very sensitive," Clarke told Auntie Anne. "She was so excited about her new look, and I wasn't sure about the change so, I said something dumb like she looked like she'd stuck her finger in a light socket. I was joking, but you know how sensitive girls are at that age. Well, I guess I knocked all the wind right out of her sails. I felt terrible about it Auntie Anne, and now I discover that I did more. I robbed her of the joy of her own self confidence." Clarke paused, deeply distraught over this memory. "Auntie Anne, how does a father recognize the joy of discovery?"

"It's in the eyes, Clarke. Look at their eyes. There will be a glow of excitement. The eyes cannot lie. When your Sissy, Wendy or Clarke Jr. come to you with excitement and joy written on their faces, make sure you guard your tongue and tone. Try to measure your response according to the excitement on the child's face. If something has to be fixed, do it after the excitement has passed, and do it gently. But don't try to fix it when they come to you with eyes that are bright, a face that is beaming, and a magnolia bud in their hands."

With that last sentence, Auntie Anne rose and made her way to the sink. She dampened a few paper towels, wiped up the mess Missy made, and threw the towels away.

"See? Everything's fine now." She said looking at both her guests. "If you fail your kids in their moments of discovery, or their joy of sharing, you lose more than the moment. You lose your children's confidence in sharing their great discoveries with the most important people in their world, Dad and Mom. Don't rob your children of their joy in their moments, lest you rob yourself of their confidence in the future."

~ The Importance of Giving Children the Freedom to Fail ~

"There you have it," Mia announced. She placed *voice* on the board, using up her last letters.

"You're out Mia?" Clarke asked doubting it happened.

"I am, so add up that score husband dear."

Auntie Anne and Clarke subtracted the points of their remaining letters from their final score. He sighed. "Well girls, you did it. Auntie Anne gets the gold, Mia, you get the silver, and I came in last.

"Oh Hon, say you won the bronze. That sounds better than 'coming in last'… although," a grin began to appear on Mia's face. "You did come in last." Mia's smile turned into a cute chuckle which she immediately harnessed with fingers pressed to her lips.

"Thank you for your words of encouragement my dear wife," Clarke retorted. "Hey Auntie Anne, how about a rematch someday?"

"We could do that, Clarke. Just give me a ring whenever you plan on being in town. You both did very well though."

While Auntie Anne cleared the table of mugs and pie plates, Mia stepped behind Clarke's chair. Leaning over she wrapped her arms around him and gently patted his arms. Clarke was encouraged. There had been something almost religious about this experience and now he didn't want to leave this sanctuary.

"I'm finding it hard to leave, Auntie Anne," he said. "You've comforted and encouraged in ways I wasn't expecting. The day has been enlightening. I hope this won't be the last time."

"Oh, I surely hope it won't be either," Auntie Anne replied. "But before you go, I have something for you, a little reminder of our day together." Auntie Anne went into the large, sunlit room beyond the kitchen. Clarke and Mia followed, feeling like the Tin Man and Dorothy on the yellow brick road. They turned the corner and stepped back in time. There they noticed Auntie's Anne's favorite cushioned armchair, covered in a treasured worn and faded quilt. The walls were a soft yellow, covered here and there with framed sketches of fruit and gardens, the works of Auntie Anne's hand. "I keep my

African violets over here near this window," she said. "They need the morning sun to grow best."

The multicolored pots sat on a low table. "All you need to grow these plants is soil. Stick a leaf in the soil and let it take root. Please pick one out for yourselves. I would like you to have it as a reminder of our wonderful day together."

"They're beautiful Auntie Anne," Mia said, "but I can't promise you that it will be alive in a few days. My father had a green thumb, but I guess I got a recessive gene because my thumb's black. My dad said I tend to kill plants. Once in the sixth grade, we had a garden project at school. You know, where all the kids get a bunch of seeds to grow in a cup, and then write a paper on the plants. My seeds never sprouted. And it's not just plants. I had goldfish a couple of times but they never survived very long. My dad said I had a knack at killing them too. He advised me to stay away from living things, so now I don't even try to grow anything. I just don't have much luck."

"It's true, Auntie Anne," Clarke said. "Just before Mia and I were married, her father warned me that I would be lucky to be alive in six months."

At this, Auntie Anne gave a hearty laugh, shaking her head in disbelief. "Well, at least that hasn't happened, yet."

Mia stood silently, looking defeated. She turned her eyes back to Auntie Anne. By all outward appearances, Mia was a woman who had it together. But her sleek, put-together-image was a dress-up costume disguising something else.

Auntie Anne smiled at her. "Mia, may I ask you a question?"

Mia gave an approving shrug and a nod of her head.

"Do you know how much a full grown elephant weighs?"

Mia turned to Clarke with a questioning look. What did elephants have to do with African violets? Turning back to Auntie Anne she said hesitantly, "No, I don't know." A cautious grin came on here face. "Is this a joke or a trick question?"

"Oh, no, its not. But full-grown African elephants weigh over twelve thousand pounds and they can grow twenty-four feet long and thirteen feet tall." Auntie Anne rattled the facts off like a talking encyclopedia.

"That is a lot of elephant to harness," Clarke said with a contemplative look.

"Oh yes Clarke, and they are strong too. Very strong!"

"And they have good memories. . . well I read that someplace," Mia added not wanting to be left out of the conversation but not exactly sure what the conversation was about.

"Now Mia, you would think animals that big would have the freedom to go wherever they please. But in the circus they stay put because one of their legs is attached by a slender rope to a very small pin driven into the ground."

Clarke heard enough to know that Auntie Anne wasn't just making small talk. Another life lesson was unfolding. "That's pretty amazing when you think about it," he said. "Here's a six-ton animal tethered to a stake in the ground that he could easily pull up. So, why doesn't he just walk off?"

"Mia touched on the reason earlier. Elephants have good memories. When they're just babies, trainers place an iron shackle and chain on one leg and then attach it to a heavy metal stake fixed in the ground. Every time that baby moves, the chain starts to cut into his hide. Eventually the baby learns that if he stands still, the chain won't hurt. Later the trainer substitutes a rope for the chain and a wooden stake is substituted for the metal one. The elephant's memory does the rest. You see, Mia, the elephant isn't really shackled to the stake; his mind is shackled to a memory, and that's what keeps him from moving."

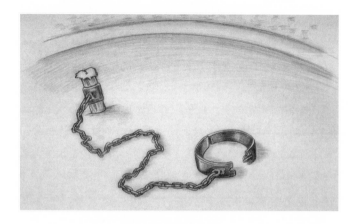

"It seems so simple when you explain it like that," Mia said. "Shackled to some memory of failure that could be popped out in a heartbeat with almost no effort."

"That's the point Mia and it is one that you need to understand. Everyone has a green thumb. It's just that some people have been told otherwise so many times by an influential person in their lives, that they believe the lie and it paralyzes them. Failures shackle their minds, and they don't step out and try again."

Auntie Anne paused just for a moment to measure her words. Clearly she had hit on something in Mia's past that needed further encouragement.

"Mia, the fear of failure is much like the fear of anything. It is faith in the wrong thing that holds you back from doing what is right, best, or possible."

Clarke realized the full implications of Auntie Anne's words. This entire conversation was not about African violets or African elephants; it was about shackling the mind with the fear of failure. A powerful shackle, holding people back from enjoying even the fun things of life, like growing flowers. "Wow, there is quite a lesson here Auntie Anne," Clarke said.

"There is Clarke! A lesson for all of us." Auntie Anne turned to meet Mia's defeated eyes. With gentle persuasion she spoke as a mother to a daughter. "My dear Mia, all you need to do is water your plant a little, and give it some morning sunlight. Just because you failed as a child, doesn't mean you will fail as an adult."

"This day has been too much for my brain," Mia confessed, plopping herself down in the white wicker rocker and propping her head in her hands. "Auntie Anne, everything seems tied back to some form of competition."

Clarke sat down on the matching wicker couch and looked at his wife. "What are you saying, Mia?"

"I'm saying that my ability to take care of this beautiful plant is competing with my fear of failing to keep it alive. My desire to have a dozen of these around the house is competing with my father's words, 'You kill everything.'"

"It's a flimsy rope shackle, Mia. There's nothing hold-ing you back but your fear of trying. Maybe there's another lesson here," Auntie Anne continued while tak-ing a seat next to Clarke on the couch. Missy jumped up and curled herself next to her mistress. Auntie Anne began to speak while slowing stroking Missy's side.

"I'm no counselor or therapist, but I do know the value of giving children the freedom to fail. A father or mother's wrong attitude toward failure can prevent chil-dren from stretching themselves and testing the limits of their giftedness. They would rather hold back, achiev-ing only enough to get by than face their parent's dissatisfaction if they fail. Your children need to know that you view their failure as the first step to success. Discouraging words during times of failures create the shackles that hold children back from enjoying life to its fullest. Wise is the parent," Auntie Anne said look-ing over to catch Clarke's eyes before continuing, "espe-cially a dad, who never takes away the sunshine because he sees a few dead leaves on the plant."

Auntie Anne rose, excused herself, and headed back toward the kitchen with Missy trotting behind. Mia and Clarke lingered for a moment to select an African vio-let. While they were looking over the colorful pots bursting with bloom, Clarke thought back to one particular day in the life of his son.

He had been replacing a hinge on the gate to the side yard. Clarke Jr. had wanted to help, so Clarke told him he could put in the screws and handed him his screw gun. Young Clarke didn't get the angle right and stripped the head of the screw. "Here, son," Clarke said. "Let me do it. I guess you just don't have a mechanical bent." Since then, Clarke Jr. hadn't shown any interest in learning to use tools. Now Clarke wondered how many other times he had jumped on his son's little failures only to have instilled big fears of failure instead. He hung his head shamefully.

Mia selected a plant, bright and beautiful. "Clarke, this flower represents a new beginning for us. It will be a memorial of our day with Auntie Anne."

Clarke took a mental inventory of the day's lessons. The danger of competing values, the need to belong, the importance of words, words like "great family" and "glad we're together." Hugs, lots more hugs, and personal handwritten notes filled with encouraging sentiments. Embracing failures and guarding his tongue and his tone. So much was learned, but now it all seems obvious. Smiling, he reached out to put his arm around his dear wife, his life partner.

Mia breathed a sigh of contentment. They had come to this stranger for some crumbs of wisdom and were pushing themselves away from a banquet table.

"Auntie Anne, we've kept you long enough," Mia said. "You must be ready for your evening meal and some time to rest. We'll be going now."

The three of them retraced their steps through the great room to the entryway.

With her arms extended, Mia moved toward Auntie Anne and embraced her. A gesture that was more of thanks than a sign of departure. As she pulled back to look into Auntie Anne's face, Mia's eyes filled up with tears. Reaching in her pocket for a tissue, she saw her brown mules by the large basket of slippers. "Oh, my!" she said. "I almost left the house wearing slippers! They're so comfortable I forgot I had them on. It's as if you knit them just for me, Auntie Anne."

"I did Mia," Auntie Anne said. "And now I want you to take them home with you."

Clarke looked at the large sweetgrass basket resting on the deacon's bench.

This did not go unnoticed by Auntie Anne. She lifted the basket and held it up before Clarke. "All these baskets are fashioned by the caring hand of a mother," she said. "But what about the father's touch, Clarke?

Has it been lost to competing values?"

Clarke stood still for a moment, and then slowly put both of his hands before his eyes and examined them like a master carpenter examining a fine piece of wood. "These hands can craft nothing at all, or they can craft something as sturdy as your front steps and as beautiful as this basket. Today, I've learned how to build a bridge to my children and how to weave trust into their lives. The beauty is in the details of every plank and every weave, and the power is in the touch. Right, Auntie Anne?"

"In a father's personal touch," she said. "Don't forget hand-holding, arms around the shoulder, and gentle pats on the back just to say, 'well done.' Several times a day, seven days a week."

Clarke put his long arms around Auntie Anne and their eyes met. "You have the eyes of a prophet, Auntie Anne. You look beyond appearances into the heart of things, and you see what's right and true. Thank you so much for sharing your insights with us."

"Well, I'm always glad to have opportunity to chat a little about what life has taught me."

Long shadows were falling over the brick walkway, and the Ligustrum leaves were shimmering in the dew. Stepping onto the front porch, Clarke gave a controlled stretch while Mia turned again toward the little woman. Taking her hand, she whispered, "Thank you, Auntie Anne, for opening our eyes to what it really means to be a trusting parent in today's untrusting world." The couple moved down the steps. They turned again to wave, and Auntie Anne raised her hand in reply.

The car was out of sight when Auntie Anne looked down at Missy and said, "All right, my sweet precious, what should we have for dinner tonight?"

Missy put her front paws on Auntie Anne's leg and whimpered.

"Okay, I get the message. You need a hug first, don't you?" She reached down, picked up the little dog, and cuddled her in her arms. "By the way," she said, "Have I told you lately how great it is to have a puppy like you in the family?"

Bringing it Home
Questions for the Heart

1. Clarke asked Auntie Anne the following question. "How can a value which is intrinsically good become bad?" What was her answer?

2. How do the good values of science, technology and marketplace economics impact your child's toy box? What was Auntie Anne's point?

3. Auntie Anne said: "It's the pansies poking through a sidewalk that packs the punch. And that's what every father must stay mindful of." What point was she making as it relates to fathering/mothering? List a few examples.

4. "Words go where we can't always be." What point was Auntie Anne making with this statement and what did she encourage Clarke to do?

5. Auntie Anne told Clarke, "When your Sissy, Wendy or Clarke Jr. come to you with excitement and joy written on their faces, make sure you guard your tongue and tone when you say something. Try to measure your response according to the excitement on the child's face." What was the lesson being communicated?

6. Auntie Anne spoke of the shackles of the mind. What are they, where do they come from, and which ones might you be dealing with?

7. "Fear is faith in the wrong thing." What are the implications of this statement in your own life?